Penny Thoughts

FOR THE HOMESCHOOLER

BE INSPIRED TO LOVE YOUR HOMESCHOOL JOURNEY

MARY KAY SMITH

Also by Mary Kay Smith:

Wings Over Zululand

This book and its contents are protected under the copyright laws of the United States.
All rights are reserved to the copyright holder(s).
Distribution without prior written authorization is prohibited.

Penny Thoughts for the Homeschooler
Copyright 2022 Mary Kay Smith

ISBN: 9781959544012

Photo Credits:

Cover photo by Kevin Dinneen
p. 48, 55, 123: photos by Ashley Taylor
p. 77: photo by Tyler Stauffer
p. 8, 19, 31, 33, 36, 47, 56, 74, 96, 112: stock photos by Adobe Stock, Shutterstock, Pixabay
All other photos by Mary Kay Smith

Penny Thoughts for the Homeschooler is a special publication of
Wootton Major Publishing
Austin, TX

This edition printed & distributed through KDP

Design by Ashley Taylor Creative

PennyThoughtsMKS@gmail.com

Penny Thoughts for the Homeschooler breathes wonder into the art and practice of homeschooling. It is anything but "penny thoughts," however; I found the encouragement, advice, support, and enthusiasm to be pure gold—Mary Kay understands homeschoolers. Like me, you'll probably find it impossible to read these devotions one at a time. The richness of each essay will compel you to keep reading, but try to space them out as much as you can for the full effect.

Gary Thomas, author of *Sacred Marriage* and *Sacred Parenting*

Mary Kay Smith delights, encourages, exhorts, and equips homeschool families through her real-life-inspired essays. HEAV's homeschooling magazine, considered one of the best in the country thanks to Mary Kay's leadership, has become a model for other state homeschool organizations. Her excellent, relevant writing makes our readers laugh, cry, and think.

Anne Miller, President, Home Educators Association of Virginia (HEAV)

Mary Kay's short essays offer nuggets of wisdom and encouragement for homeschooling parents through vignettes and simple, home-like images. Her experience and kind heart shine through.

Kathy Kuhl, author, speaker, coach (LearnDifferently.com)

Mary Kay is one of the precious women who kept me on track and encouraged me throughout my sixteen years of homeschooling. She is insightful and knowledgeable and has a vast array of ideas to make school fun and engaging. Her book is winsome and engaging, and you will find comfort and wisdom here to keep you going. The chapters are short, yet poignant, and I know you will be heartened and blessed by the memoirs of this beautiful woman.

Diana Campbell, contributing author, *The Virginia Home Educator*

Homeschooling can be joyous but hard. Homeschooling moms are often haunted by fearful thoughts that undermine our confidence in what we are doing. Mary Kay's book is a balm for those fears. She gives great encouragement in homeschooling—that you can give your children what they need to succeed and that what you are doing is good. She shares practical advice, anecdotes, and reminders of the joys to be found in homeschooling. Pick it up and read a few pages when you are feeling down, and it will give you the confidence not to give up.

Paula Inglis, homeschool speech and debate coach

Mary Kay's writing for homeschoolers is fabulous—encouraging, real, articulate, experienced.

Vicki Bentley, author, speaker, consultant for Home School Legal Defense Association

For my children, Jason, Lindsey, and Ashley,
who made homeschooling easy, interesting, and fun.

For my husband, Brad,
who willingly, unwaveringly supported us
in the homeschool journey.

I'm proud of you all; I love you all!

Contents

INTRODUCTION
The Promise of Homeschooling — 9

WHY HOMESCHOOL?
Hidden Crystals — 12
Kept Woman — 14
Gardenia — 16
The Homeschool Bubble — 18
Innovative Building — 20

FINDING SUPPORT
Support Groups — 26
Don't Let Go of the Pole — 30
Easy Enough for Anyone — 32
Lost Along the Ginza — 34
Interrupted Plans — 36

KNOWING WHERE YOU'RE GOING
Pena Palace — 40
Creating a Cozy School — 42
Getting Directions — 46
Preparedness — 48
Chewing a Box — 50
Volunteering — 52
Home-Based Business — 54
Waiting for Godot — 56

MAKING THE JOURNEY EASIER
Distilled Life — 60
Organization — 62
Dads and Homeschooling — 64

Milk and Cookie Parenting	66
Relaxing into Preschool	68
The Adventure of Homeschooling	70
Staying Focused	74
Practical Science	76
Living with Enthusiasm	78
Second Chances	80
Keeping Your Armor Cleaned	84

ADVICE ALONG THE WAY

Thundering Displays	88
Smoking Mountains	90
Thinking Like an Israelite	94
Impacting the Culture	96
Journaling	100
Crumbling Stones	102
African Bush	104
High Places	110
Architecture	112
Pointing the Camera	114

FINAL THOUGHTS

Life After Homeschooling	122
Transitions	124

ACKNOWLEDGEMENTS   127

ABOUT THE AUTHOR   129

THE *Promise* OF HOMESCHOOLING

I was newly married when I first heard about homeschooling. A family moved into the community who had three cute school-aged kids they carted everywhere, many times with books in tow. The children were fun-loving, well-behaved, and smart, and it wasn't too long before our conversations led to the family's school choice. They introduced me to Raymond and Dorothy Moore and their books *Home Grown Kids* and *Better Late Than Early*.

I was hooked! The arguments for homeschooling made sense, and I loved the idea. My husband and I agreed we would do it—and I was not even pregnant.

It helped that I was not at all concerned about the (at that time) unorthodox approach, as I had some unconventional schooling myself. I spent my junior school (elementary) years at a boarding school in South Africa, but I did most of my high school work by correspondence courses from an American university, the overstuffed airmail envelopes winging their way back and forth across the Atlantic. And then I went to college without even finishing the high school program. After I completed my first year, the college arranged an automatic Regents high school diploma for me. So I knew that alternative schooling worked just fine.

I had such fun pouring through the immensely helpful *The Big Book of Home Learning* by Mary Pride and making curriculum choices and placing orders when we were ready to start several years later!

Now, homeschoolers have co-ops, Google, chat rooms, and Facebook to find information—not to mention conventions, where you can hear speakers on every conceivable related topic and view curricula, math manipulatives, science equipment, books, DVDs, and just plain fun stuff first-hand.

How exciting! A new year ahead. Blank pages, sharpened pencils, fresh ideas, new plans. I'm just as thrilled about the promises of homeschooling today as I was more than thirty years ago, and obviously others agree, as I continue to see more families opt for this schooling method.

I'm so happy that you have decided to join in.

WHY HOMESCHOOL?

Hidden Crystals

When I was growing up, my family would occasionally set out for another ridge on our mountain to hunt for amethysts. My father showed us what to look for: large, round, grey rocks with pitted surfaces. Whenever we thought we found one, he would hit it hard with his hammer. If it really was a geode, it would split immediately, and if we were lucky, we'd be treated to the thrilling sight of dazzling purple and white crystals in the hollow center.

One year, I took one of my amethysts to Kenya where I taught underprivileged children for two weeks—one in a rural mountain orphanage school and the other in the Kibera slum of Nairobi. I showed the kids the rough, pitted side of the stone, and they couldn't figure out why I had bothered to bring something that ugly from South Africa to the United States and then to Kenya. Then I flipped the stone over. Their mouths dropped open when they caught sight of the gorgeous, glittering crystals inside. Raw amethysts are a wonderful object lesson—a picture of the sparkle, colors, and fascinating formations that are inside us, waiting to be revealed.

In Kenya, we talked quite a bit about David and Joseph and the skills they developed when they were young that came into play when they became rulers. David and Joseph might have thought their lives looked like the boring shell of the geode, but God knew what was hidden that He wanted to use later.

While I was trying to encourage these children that God could see beyond *their* current circumstances, too, to the sparkle beneath, it struck me once again how absolutely blessed homeschoolers are because we already get that idea. We *look* for the colors and flickering in our kids to see how God has gifted them. We help them get the education and training they need to bring that shine out. We encourage the sometimes painful character polishing to bring out their true gemlike qualities. What a privilege for us to participate in something so wonderful!

So the next time someone asks you why you homeschool, just show them a picture of an amethyst. We're bringing out our kids' cut, color, clarity, and spark to show God's glory.

KEPT *Woman*

One day I passed a group of women talking about stay-at-home moms and overheard one of them say scornfully, "Well, *I* certainly didn't expect or want to be a **kept woman!**"

I almost laughed out loud. What a ridiculous notion. Let's see: housekeeper, chef, laundress, seamstress, decorator, gardener, chauffeur, shopper, nanny, nurse, counselor...so many professions in the role of a homemaker, and when you add homeschool teacher, records keeper, and guidance counselor in there (for *how* many subjects, *how* many grades, *how* many years?), the list jumps substantially. Just think how much money and frustration we're saving our families by caring for them ourselves! "Kept women" we most definitely are not.

I happen to think homeschooling is fun. My own children are grown, but after they graduated, I got to work with my nephews and later with other children. We were always learning something new. One day we read about Dizzie Gillespie, so we looked him up on YouTube. His cheeks really did puff out when he played! Another day, we checked to see what ptarmigans looked like. We learned Hawaiian vocabulary, cooked Swedish food, gazed awestruck at petunia petals under a microscope, and wrote funny limericks. We discussed ice skating lessons and Civil Air Patrol meetings and how expensive it is to keep a parakeet.

As a homeschool mom—or, in my case later, aunt and tutor—we are privileged to be not just part of the children's school, but of their life. We hear what they think, sympathize with their frustrations, and share their excitements and dreams.

One of the best parts of being with the kids so much, and in the casual environment of a home school, is the opportunity to have "God discussions" at the drop of a hat.

One time, I had a vase of my carpet roses on the table. They were gorgeous, with dark pink outer petals that faded to a beautiful, delicate peach inside.

As the morning progressed, some of the petals began to fall onto the table. The boys decided they would arrange those petals around the vase like a wreath, since the petals were still pretty and soft.

The next day, though, the petals had withered and shrunk to half their size; their edges were curled and starting to go brown. The boys were both fascinated and disappointed by the rapid rate of decomposition. But, that gave me the perfect object lesson and opportunity to discuss the principle and application of abiding in the vine from John 15!

Of course, in order to have good "God discussions," we homeschoolers need to be Bible scholars too. So add that to the list!

Being the keeper of your home and children is a full time job and ministry and money-saver wrapped into one. Don't ever let anyone talk down to you because you stay at home. We are not kept women—our value is far above rubies... literally!

Gardenia

Yesterday a flower fell off my gardenia bush. That would have been fine if it had gone through its normal cycle, opening its beautiful, soft, cream-colored petals and releasing its dramatic fragrance, but it hadn't. It wasn't old and spent. Instead, the bud had grown and almost opened but then dried and shriveled without ever doing what it was meant to do, what I had been looking forward for it to do.

It happened because I was away for three weeks. I left watering instructions, but there were three different people involved, and somehow the amounts or the times weren't right, and my plant apparently didn't get enough water.

The thing is, this plant is picky for some reason. I don't get a lot of flowers from it, so each one is very special. I know its character and symptoms, and I watch it vigilantly. There have been times I've had to spray or painstakingly wash every leaf to get rid of mites. There have been times I've had to give it more or less water. There have been times I've had to prune dead parts away. Even though I am not a perfect caretaker for this gardenia, I know it well and really want it to flourish. Because of that, I can do a better job of taking care of it than anyone else.

It occurred to me that our kids are like that gardenia, and homeschooling parents are like its caretaker.

As teachers we might not have teacher training or know every option for curriculum that is out there. But we know our kids the best and can make adjustments as we see what works and what doesn't in their learning.

As parents we might not do everything correctly all the time, but we love our kids the most and have the incentive to make adjustments as we see what works and what doesn't in their maturity, spiritual growth, and happiness.

The ones who not only have their children's best interest at heart, but observe closely and know them well are the ones best qualified to take care of them. Even in our weaknesses, we are really the best caretakers for our kids because we have the personal connection and flexibility that even wonderful classroom teachers just can't have.

So, as you start a new school year or continue into one, don't be concerned that your kids are missing something better. They are not. They might be missing something different, but that is not the same thing. Your love and individual attention to them is what matters most.

THE HOMESCHOOL BUBBLE

A friend whose son I had been working with was once very angry with me for resigning my position. After she talked about all the things she didn't like, she delivered the final blow: "...and you homeschool your children, too!"

While I was pondering what this had to do with anything, she continued, "You are raising your children in a bubble. What good will they ever be to the world?" It was the old socialization argument in disguise.

It's true that this woman had sent her own children to public school, but what was more fascinating to me wasn't the argument of homeschool versus public school, but that this Christian who knew the Bible well thought learning and life preparation doesn't take place in bubbles.

Really?

It seems to me that Moses' first wilderness experience was a bubble. Forty years of it! I think he learned a few more lessons about humility and true leadership during that quiet, isolated time than in his previous years in the "world" of the palace. That wilderness bubble probably taught him a few practical skills he'd need later, too.

What could be more of an isolation bubble than spending your days with sheep? Yet David must have used that time to work on his scientific skills—understanding the nature and care of sheep; his warrior skills—using a slingshot and killing with his hands; as well as his artistic skills—playing the harp and writing poetry. Wow! A Renaissance man before the Renaissance, a king chosen by God, a man after God's own heart—prepared in a bubble.

Paul's three years in the Arabian Desert mentioned in Galatians 2 qualifies as bubble training too, I would think. And look at the impact he made!

So, don't ever be concerned about being in a homeschool bubble. It's even okay if that's on someone's list of why she doesn't like you. In-depth learning, creativity, and character formation take place away from distractions. Use your bubble to form leaders, thinkers, creators, and children after God's own heart. When they emerge, watch out world!

Tip

Want to raise "Renaissance Kids"? Teach them skills, and give them an education and experience in many fields of study. Teach music along with a sport. Teach art along with science. Teach history along with Bible. Teach economics along with godly character. Teach truth. Teach compassion. Teach God.

Innovative BUILDING

On a recent trip to Switzerland, my husband and I toured the Ballenberg Open Air Museum—163 acres of hilly, wooded countryside displaying more than 100 residential and farm buildings that represent every region of Switzerland from the 14th to the 19th centuries.

We peeked inside the different buildings and watched various demonstrations of smithing, weaving, carving, cheese-making, etc., and I was struck that it all looked very familiar. I suddenly realized that's because 500 years later, people were still doing things the same way. Yes, the chalet shape was unique, but if you go to Williamsburg, Claude Moore Farm, Sully Plantation, or any of our other Virginia colonial sites, you'll find that people were still doing things much as before, and the homes, farm houses, and overall way of life was pretty much unchanged. As a friend of ours would say tongue in cheek, "That is 500 years unencumbered by progress."

"We've always done it that way" is a familiar phrase to us all, but aren't we thankful for those innovative people who eventually change some of

that? I'm certainly thrilled to have a house with a strong foundation, indoor bathrooms, insulated walls, electricity, and kitchen and laundry appliances. I'm also thankful for inoculations, modern hospitals, paved roads, cars… I am thankful that someone—really, many "someones"—figured out that the old ways could be improved upon.

That is exactly what homeschooling has done for education.

We don't have to send our kids to sit quietly in rows to learn exactly and only what the state requires and tests. Our kids don't have to learn from only one teaching style or listen to the teacher's personal philosophy of life even when it disagrees with ours. We have improved on all that. We can teach what we believe to be important; we can teach during the hours our kids are most alert; we can tutor one on one or participate in a co-op; we can add courses to encourage our kids' strengths.

We have not allowed ourselves to be "unencumbered" by taking the easy, familiar way, but instead we have chosen the hard work of making our own selections and directing our kids' schooling ourselves. No, it has not been effortless for any of us, but that's exactly why the result has been progress.

How wonderful that we are not part of a museum with air space between the logs, cracks in the floorboards, and an outhouse out back. Instead, we have been building on a new, strong schooling foundation for our children!

FINDING SUPPORT

Support Groups

This morning I sat by my kitchen window to observe my backyard wildlife habitat in action. I watched fascinated as one bird after another zoomed in for breakfast...juncos, finches, starlings, doves, blue jays, redwing blackbirds. A fat red-bellied woodpecker flew to one suet feeder while starlings squabbled at another. Finches took advantage of the fighting to dart around and steal dropped seeds, but Mrs. Cardinal, with her orange lipstick and perfect coiffure, waited in the pear tree for her turn, like the proper lady she is. It's no wonder God blessed the birds when He created them—they provide such *diversion!*

Suddenly a shadow flew over and all the birds

darted into the Leylands. Thirty or more birds just disappeared, leaving nothing for the predator. I thought—this is habitat at work! This is why a habitat not only has to provide food, water, and a place to raise young, but also cover—a place of safety. And the interesting thing is when birds go to that place of safety, all differences of habit, preferences of style, and old squabbles disappear. They huddle together with a common purpose.

I think support groups are one of the types of cover for homeschoolers. As families we choose different curricula, approach education in unique ways, have different-style homes and clothing, worship in various churches...but put us in a support group and we lay those differences aside to help one another, encourage one another, and pray for one another.

Sometimes we just need information or people to share resources with. But other times we struggle with difficult issues in our home or schooling and need someone to remind us that, no matter what long-term goals any of us have, it's really just one step at a time.

In *The Lord of the Rings* story, where would Frodo have been without Sam? Sam consistently provided cover for Frodo—sometimes literally pulling him away from danger, and other times just encouraging him. As he tells Frodo when they're exhausted near the end of their long quest, "We have to get down there, there's nothing for it. Let's just make it down the next hill for starters."

We all need that kind of support person or group—someone who will look us in the eye when we're thinking of giving up and say as Sam did: "Don't you let go. Please don't let go...*Reach!*"

How about you? Is there cover in your homeschool habitat—or are you easy prey for the shadows?

Tip

You can register your backyard as a wildlife habitat with the National Wildlife Federation if you provide food, cover, water, and a place for wildlife to raise their young. My own yard is certified, and I led my town's five-year effort to register as a community wildlife habitat. (www.nwf.org/Garden-for-Wildlife/Certify)

DON'T LET GO OF THE POLE

A friend told me recently about her son's pole-vaulting event. During one of his practices, he used a much bigger and stronger pole than usual to get over the twelve-foot bar. He missed and started to fall backwards from midair. Now, the cardinal rule of pole vaulting is that if you fall, you never let go of the pole because that is what will bring you down safely. So, as soon as they saw him start to fall backwards, both of his coaches and all his teammates started yelling, "Don't let go of the pole! Don't let go of the pole!" He remembered his training; he listened to his teammates, and he landed safely.

When I heard this story, I thought of the time my son fell off a raft when he was white-water rafting with his church youth group. The group had been trained on what to do if that should happen, and as his head came up out of the water, he looked for the raft and saw all of his teammates pointing left to where he needed to swim to avoid the rafting lane. Eventually, with God's help, he emerged in a calm stretch between rapids and saw the raft waiting not ten yards away. A member of the group extended an oar towards him and helped him clamber back aboard.

Without a team, adventures can quickly become tragedies. We all need our friends to remind us what to do when we falter. They remind us of our goals and plans. They help us recognize what is real and to know which end is up. They help us regain perspective. They encourage us to hang onto God's truths. They help us get where we want to go.

If you haven't yet, find some people who will remind you not to let go of the pole or who will show you where to swim to avoid dangers and find calm water again.

"A person standing alone can be attacked and defeated, but two can stand back-to-back and conquer. Three are even better, for a triple-braided cord is not easily broken."

(Ecclesiastes 4:12, NLT)

Easy Enough FOR ANYONE

The brochures about Diamond Head said the hike was "easy enough that almost anyone could do it." Besides, it was just more than a mile round trip. Sounded good—and who is going to give up the opportunity to hike up an extinct volcano in Hawaii?

After about my third stop to ease my pounding heart, I said to my son, "Well, sure I can do it, but I'm surprised they didn't say anything about the hike being a real workout!" He responded, "They figured the word 'hike' was enough to scare off most of the sedentary population—we are what's left, and for people who hike a lot, it *is* easy."

One thing I knew for sure—if I wanted to get to the top, it was up me to me to get there; the summit was not going to come down to me.

That principle may be obvious about a hike, but it wasn't so obvious to me about parenting. I didn't understand it fully until I read Gary Thomas's book *Sacred Parenting*—a book I highly recommend.

When we are tempted to give up, Gary reminds us that the opposite of love is apathy; love is about your movement *toward* someone. So, if you want to reach the summit with your kids—no matter what their ages—*you* have to keep going toward them; don't expect them to come to you.

Did you think "It's so easy almost anyone can do it" about homeschooling or parenting? Have you been surprised by the continual hard work along the way, or faced disappointing results? Maybe we were using the wrong measuring stick. Sometimes disappointment has to do with our expectations; sometimes it has to do with our failures; sometimes it has to do with our children not understanding or taking consequences seriously.

But don't give up hope. As our former pastor used to say, "The last chapter isn't written yet." We have this promise from Philippians 1:6: "He that began a good work in you will perform it until the day of Jesus Christ." That's a good reminder for you; it's a good one for your kids.

The peak awaits—let's keep going.

Lost Along the Ginza

One summer my family led a children's and youth program for missionary kids in Japan's famous mountain retreat, Karuizawa. We had an afternoon off work and our host drove us to do some souvenir shopping at the charming town square on the street affectionately known as the "Ginza"—the name borrowed from Tokyo's high-end shopping thoroughfare. We had walked to the Ginza from the language school where we were staying one other time, so we knew it was only a short way back, and thought we could easily find our way.

To our homeschooling family, the Ginza was a whole fantastic Japanese field trip in itself. We trailed through shops selling traditional clothing and wooden kokeshi dolls. In the antique store we browsed through hand-sewn rice paper books, old china, and World War II Imperial Japanese Navy Air Force uniforms. In the cat store we learned the reason the Maneki Neko cats from the Edo era have one paw up (a beckoning gesture depicting wishes for prosperity). At the modern ice cream café, we were fascinated with the flavor options of corn soup, bean, sweet potato, black sesame, or cherry blossom. We also saw the Japanese version of KFC, with a large statue of the colonel wearing a kimono! We had a great time exploring and learning!

Well, the girls and I had to return early to attend

a meeting, so our party split up. We set forth up and down the Ginza, trying side roads, turning around, starting again, and trying other side roads...but never finding our way. Finally with sore feet and an aching back, and with the meeting already well under way without us, I said, "That's it! I'm going back to the square and just finding a seat. Someone will eventually notice we're missing, come along and spot us, and lead us home."

The "someone" was my son, Jason. He and my husband strolled across our path, and Jason pointed to a street we had walked past four times. "That's our road right there, don't you remember?" he asked. "If you look up at the top, you can see the tea room where we have to turn right in order to get back." Sure enough, there it was. The problem was, it didn't look the same from this angle. But my son, being the good Eagle Scout he is, had remembered his wilderness training and was the only one who had thought to turn around on the way down and see what the view looked like from the other direction!

I think school years can be like this. We can have wonderful learning experiences and great field trips and then "get lost" and become tired, trying to feel our way through the rest of the year or in planning

for the next one.

It helps to turn around. Look at the view from the other direction. Notice where you have been and how far you have come. And most of all don't walk alone. Find someone who can point out a different perspective and get you back on the right road.

Tip

When you want to help someone, don't just ask them vaguely to let you know if they need anything. Instead, offer specific help, such as arranging dinners several times a week, doing their laundry each Friday, or driving their kids to their activities.

INTERRUPTED *Plans*

There are still six pages of e-mails in the folder I set up for a mission trip to Zambia. E-mails that told me my CBD books were on their way and my Oriental Trading order had shipped. E-mails from Precepts Ministry informing me that they were donating Bible study pamphlets and from the American Bible Society saying they were agreeing to send Bibles along. E-mails from national pastors expressing excitement about our coming, e-mails confirming our flights, and e-mails from friends saying they wanted to support us.

I have a huge file of the lesson plans I took months to prepare and the ideas I had for presenting them. My passport sported extra pages, my visa from my previous trip was still valid, and my inoculations were complete. I was thoroughly and completely ready for that trip—the one I didn't get to take.

Instead, I gave my daughters a quick crash course, turning them from my helpers into the trainers of national children's ministry leaders, sent them off with my husband who was training national pastors, and I tearfully stayed home to recuperate from unexpected back surgery.

Have your plans been interrupted?

Many people set out to homeschool with a path all laid out. Their research is complete, their books and supplies are organized, their schedule is planned, and their excitement is high. Then something happens. Their curriculum doesn't seem to fit their children. They find themselves dealing with morning sickness. Someone is diagnosed with a serious illness. One child needs more mom time and energy, leaving the others floundering.

How do we deal with interruptions, sickness, and changes? As for me, my mother and son both moved in to take care of me, and friends phoned and sent sympathetic notes, brought flowers and meals, and drove me where I needed to go. Those things didn't change the facts, bring my mission opportunity back, or restore me to health, but in the middle of my loss they provided encouragement and help.

If you are the one struggling, don't try to go it alone. If you're watching another family struggle, offer them encouragement and practical help. When everyone pitches in, the load feels so much lighter, and eventually you'll get back on track.

KNOWING WHERE YOU'RE GOING

Pena Palace

I had just visited the most impressively bizarre structure I had ever seen—the Palâcio de Pena in Sintra, Portugal. Staring up at it in fascination, I couldn't decide whether it would be an architect's dream or nightmare. Certainly, visitors have to pause in amazement if not admiration.

On one end, the palace is mostly square and built of red stone. It looks a bit medieval English but with Disney-Castle-like watch towers and both Roman and Gothic arches.

The next section over, the walls are rounded and covered in blue and brown embossed tiles of geometric Moorish designs. The entry way is plastered with a million shells and guarded by a huge, carved, Nordic-looking creature of myth— half man and half fish—who strains to hold up a tree growing out of his head and shoulders. Here the watch towers and turrets look like Russian onion domes and Turkish minarets.

The third section is a large, round, yellow tower with a brown, domed roof; and the final section reverts back to a more traditional castle built of yellow stone, but with two round towers and one minaret.

The only thing that the building has in common with itself is the outer battlement wall.

The inside is the same hodgepodge. Visitors roam from the Moorish courtyard whose walls and floor are completely covered with many varied tile designs of muted colors, to busy, fluffy Victorian chambers, to dark, lace-carved, wooded Indian rooms, and on and on. The place is impressively baffling.

One of my immediate random thoughts on seeing the palace was, "I would sure hate to think that I could look like that!" Or my family. Or my home school.

I'm not talking here about incorporating curriculum from a variety of sources or using different teaching styles for your different children. I don't think curriculum and activity variety is a bad thing, but you have to be careful that too much

change might end up causing your home or school to look like—well—a Pena Palace.

We can learn a lesson here: we need to know from the start why we homeschool and where we're headed so that we don't follow every latest trend that comes along. We need to remember what season of life we're in and what else besides school is happening in the family. Just because your children's friends participate in a debate group or play soccer doesn't mean yours have to.

As we talk to other families, read books, and attend conventions, it's good to see what is out there, but we need to keep our own educational and family goals in mind so we know when it's time to say, "That Moorish design *is* beautiful and seems to be perfect for you, but we're really the Roman type."

CREATING A *Cozy* SCHOOL

I attended boarding school for all of my elementary school years and part of high school. Though I enjoyed school, and my life was far from miserable, I was woken each morning by three loud buzzers, sent to breakfast by another buzzer, and went to dinner and then study hall at the sound of other buzzers. Like all the kids, I had a closet and drawers but no place, really, to decorate or display personal mementos or anything like that. The boarding hostel smelled like clean floor polish.

Well, it was school, after all—not home.

Later, when I attended college, I was back in another institution with another dormitory. There were four of us in my room freshman year, just like boarding

school. We had our own desk space, closet, and dresser, with not really room for much else. If you didn't want to study in the dorm, you could go to a library carousel. The library smelled like clean wood polish.

But, that was school, after all—not home.

So, when I chose to homeschool, the last thing I wanted was for it to "look like school". I kept my kids home for several reasons, and one reason was so they wouldn't have an institutional upbringing. I had no desire to re-create a traditional classroom. My kids (and later my nephews and others I tutored) did not sit at desks; we worked at the kitchen table. Most times we were joined by our dog and at least one bird.

We cozied up under an afghan on the family room sofa to read books. We lit scented candles. During the cold months we stopped for tea time. Each child chose a favorite china cup and enjoyed pouring from the teapot and using the claw-footed tongs to get sugar cubes. In the warm months, we sometimes did school out on the verandah, enjoying homemade mint iced tea.

That's not to say we didn't have any structure. Everyone had to be dressed and ready for the day by 9. School started on time, and we worked all morning. I did not answer the phone or allow outside distractions of any kind.

But, we did it in an inviting environment. We brought in fresh flowers from the garden. Our school smelled like jasmine or cranberry candles, maybe peach tea, sometimes homemade bread.

After school, we cleaned up and still had plenty of time to get to ballet lessons, karate, Boy Scouts, clubs, and whatever else the kids wanted to do.

Friends have often commented how "welcoming and peaceful" my home is. I used to wonder why, but finally realized that maybe it is peaceful because I don't allow clutter. There aren't dishes in the sink, piles that needed to be sorted, laundry waiting to be carried upstairs. Though it can't pass a white-glove inspection, the house generally looks as though it is ready for guests and not as though they are interrupting me in the middle of chores. Gentle music helps too.

I wanted my family to feel that, too. School time needed to feel just as warm and cozy as down time or guest time. Each morning I wanted our house to look clean and ready for the next project or adventure, not showing debris from the last three. Mess is never inviting.

Maybe you like desks in a row in front of a blackboard. That's okay. But, just know you don't have to do school that way. After all, just because you decided to school at home doesn't mean you have to make your home to look like school.

Tip

Look around you when you leave the room and teach your kids to do the same. Is it as clean and neat (or neater) as when you entered it? Clean up as you go. Don't allow clutter.

GETTING DIRECTIONS

I got into an argument with my GPS. I was in Pennsylvania driving along a well-known route when I came upon a barrier. The road simply closed. I took the forced exit and was immediately in a dilemma—no signs on what to do next or how to get back on track. So, since I was now in unfamiliar territory, I did the obvious thing: pull off the road to plug in my GPS.

The GPS thought I was in Kansas. It routed me through 1,045 miles and informed me it would take sixteen hours to arrive at my destination. A couple minutes later it found me and changed information.

Much better. Except it didn't know about the road closure. So it sent me about five miles on a country road heading in what I was pretty sure was the wrong direction. Of course, that was where I also lost my cell phone reception. Sure enough, the GPS led me back to my route—right below the place I was stopped the first time!

This time a construction worker was present at the barrier, so I joined a line of cars that must also have made my nice little loop, to ask for human directions. These worked.

On my way home I kept the GPS plugged in just in case the route was blocked the southern way as well. No problems—except when I approached Leesburg and decided to drive through the town rather than around it. Now, I have often thought my GPS would like to tell me off when I don't want to follow its directions. I am amazed that it simply says "Calculating route" rather than "Why don't you just do what I say?" or "Fine. Have it your own way, then!"

Of course, the tone of voice doesn't change and it's really not supposed to care, but this time it became insistent: "Make a legal U-turn. Go on 15 bypass."

"Make a legal U-turn. Go on 15 bypass." "Make a legal U-turn. Go on 15 bypass." Over and over. I was already way past the town, and my GPS was still directing me—backwards—to take the bypass.

I unplugged it.

You know, when you're on the road, you not only have to know your destination, but you really also have to have some idea of how to get there. It's good to map it out yourself. You want to know your direction, be able to recognize markers along the way, and find alternate routes.

Parenting and homeschooling are like that too. You have to know your objective. Plan it out. Know when and how you want to get there. Maybe there will be the occasional route change along the way, but when other voices come your way, disagreeing with you, trying to make you go backwards saying, "Make a legal U-turn; go on the bypass," you need to be able to evaluate them accurately. Is that advice really getting you where you want to go, or is it time to unplug?

Because, if you don't, maybe you really will wind up in Kansas.

Preparedness

I once read an interesting article about Joe Riley, the mayor of Charleston, South Carolina (*Southern Living*, September 2015). The writer talked about how intentional Mr. Riley had been about creating racial harmony and opportunity and building up the city's economy during his forty years as mayor.

He had two major disasters during his tenure: Hurricane Hugo in 1989, which wiped out part of the city, and the June 17 shooting at Mother Emanuel. He couldn't prevent either one, but all of his preparations paid off in both cases. Mayor Riley made an intriguing comment: *"Disasters catch you where you are, and then they accelerate your natural condition from that place."*

The Bible has something similar to say: "Therefore, be careful how you walk, not as unwise men, but as wise, making the most of your time, because the days are evil" (Ephesians 5:15 NASB).

That word "time" is "kairos." Merriam Webster defines kairos as "a time when conditions are right for the accomplishment of a crucial action: the opportune and decisive moment." If we have been walking carefully, we'll act in that decisive moment of opportunity the way we should.

This begs the questions for all of us: how intentional are we, how diligent, how ready to face whatever comes our way? This isn't just important for civil leaders but for everyone. Christian parents and homeschoolers have a particular reason to take this to heart.

Whether excitedly or reluctantly, we have chosen to educate our own children, and that choice brings major responsibilities. Have we analyzed where we are now and what holes we need to fill in our families' education, character training, and relationships? Have we been intentional about getting whatever help or resources we need? Have we been developing habits of timeliness, organization, diligence, and perseverance in ourselves and our children?

If so, when crises arise and catch us where we are—and they will—our schooling and our family life won't fall apart. We'll ride on the wave of our "natural" condition—the one we've been working on day after day up until that point.

CHEWING A BOX

I was watching my parrot the other day. She sat on a large cardboard box and chewed and yanked and ripped and did her best to tear the box apart. That same box has been in her playpen area for months and gives her great satisfaction whenever she sits there. Most of the outer layer is gone, and there are holes here and there.

All bird owners know the mantra "A chewing bird is a happy bird," but it's such a funny thing. While it may be instinctive—and she does treat her chewing with great importance—it really doesn't do her any good other than provide entertainment. It's not as though she chews a hole and then tries to nest in the box. Once it is in shreds, she wants something else. Yet, she'll sometimes hiss softly at me if I come close to her while she's working on her box, giving a gentle warning that what she's doing is way too essential to be interrupted.

Watching her, I suddenly thought of how many times we are busy like that—so full of activity, so intent, so focused, so determined not to be distracted, so sure we're doing something important, so convinced our project needs to be perfected just one tiny bit more. Perhaps we even hiss when we feel disturbed.

But maybe we're just chewing a box.

Does God ever look over at us and shake His head with a tolerant, amused smile? Or maybe a sad smile because He knows we're just "spinning wheels" and our busyness won't amount to anything? Does He know our time could be better spent or that we're trying too hard when we don't need to?

As we finish off each school year and evaluate the next, let's be sure to seek God's direction to make

certain we're focusing on the right things—for ourselves, our families, our homes, our schools. I sure don't want to get to the end of my important project and find I was just chewing a box.

An hour later, my bird was still busy. But all she had to show for it was a pile of cardboard on the counter.

Tip

You know you're trying too hard when your joy is gone, when all your focus is on one thing and you ignore other blessings in your life, and when you're getting signs from your friends and family that something isn't right with your focus.

Volunteering

What does volunteering have to do with homeschooling? Aren't we parents busy enough with the education of our families without having to add volunteering to our workload? Well, when we volunteer, we gain as much as we give.

One of the wonderful things about homeschool families volunteering together is that the children are learning by doing—they are being automatically and naturally trained as the next generation of volunteers!

My own daughters went with me to Japan and Hong Kong for a month, helping me with some children's programs. It wasn't just a nice trip for them; they worked right alongside me preparing dramas, crafts, and object lessons. They had to cope with the inconvenience of foreign travel with its inoculations, long flights, weird food, and squat toilets. But you know what? The next time it was easier. And the time after that it was easier still. And by the time they were adults they didn't think anything of preparing for and going to an unknown place for ministry.

My kids also volunteered for our town, at a local historic site, at church, and for friends.

Tip

Sometimes volunteering can turn into—or enhance—school credit. With the addition of extra (related) reading and writing assignments, voluteering at a historical site can turn into history credit, a mission trip can turn into a social studies credit, voluteering with animals at a zoo or helping at a community farm can be part of a science credit.

This is true of all other extra-curricular activities, too. Ballet or karate can count as PE, cooking and sewing can go towards home economics credit, etc.

As homeschoolers in charge of our own schedules, we can rearrange our days to participate in community service. We can carve out time to volunteer in a nursing home, fire station, homeless shelter, the zoo, or public gardens. We can rearrange our school months to accommodate mission trips or overseas volunteer work.

Sometimes you even get a return for volunteering. Steady volunteering can make a difference on a college application, it can provide the opportunity for scholarships, and it can help win awards. It can even lead to a job.

Isn't homeschooling great? We can do what we want when we want, and then tie it all together with our curriculum! And who can argue? All educators agree that hands-on learning is best! So whatever and however you do it, be sure volunteer work is part of your homeschool plan.

HOME-BASED *Business*

I wasn't sure it could be done. After all, how many wedding cakes have you seen that can be successfully transported on a head? But the request came with the assumption that this was nothing unusual, and when you are trying to be helpful and earn money as a teenager, you are reluctant to turn business away.

So I made the cake. It was three-tiered; rectangular for strength; and though it had a decorative topper, it didn't have separating pillars—I doubted the lady's skill was that good. But when she came to pick it up, she easily balanced this one on her head and walked regally away, thrilled to have a real wedding cake decorated in yellow icing roses and white icing swags for her special day.

Unless you are a milliner, I doubt you can boast that the fruit of your business has been carried away on someone's head. You also won't be able to relate to another experience of mine when our car slid along the muddy Ubombo Mountain road past chickens and goats to another wedding, my mother and brother helping me hang on to the various tiers of the cake as my dad directed, "Hold on—here comes another pothole."

But everyone in his or her own business will have some kind of story to tell.

Cake decorating didn't start out as a business for me. It was a hobby and, in fact, I only continued it as a business through high school and then turned it back to a hobby. My first wedding cake was by request, as a favor to an African pastor and his nurse wife. From there, the idea spread to his relatives and co-workers, and then beyond to someone I'd never heard of, who walked several miles through the bush to carry the cake home on her head.

Many businesses start out that way. Sometimes we forget that a skill we have acquired is marketable to anyone else. To us it is so normal. It's true that some pastimes are best left as hobbies—you don't want to "burn out" doing something you enjoy a little but not enough to work at several hours a day. But often hobbies are the beginning of successful home businesses.

Are you considering starting a home business as part of, or in addition to, your school? Many homeschool families do. Are you wondering how to choose or what's involved? Take a look at what you already know, what you can't stay away from, what others repeatedly ask you to do, and what you are interested in finding out about.

Maybe one of those options is right for you—for now, for a while, or from now on.

Tip

What about helping your children create a home-based business? My son took classes with the National Wildlife Federation (and became their youngest person to be certified as a Habitat Steward) and formed his landscaping company Yardscapes. That kept him busy and earning money all through high school as well as college summers. My two daughters took classes with Stampin' Up and started Mossflower Cards. My youngest daughter later created "Over the Hump Confections," for which she baked goodies for my husband to take to work and sell each Wednesday. What do your kids like to do?

Tip

Get up! Today! *Now!* Make your bed. Tidy up. Count your blessings. Exercise for five minutes. Dress smart. Get going.

Waiting for Godot

Do you ever feel as though you're "waiting for Godot"? You know—decide to get going, sit there, think about it; decide to get going, sit there, think about it; decide...

Sometimes as the school year continues, our energy and enthusiasm for school (or other activities) wanes a little bit. It seems as if our "starters" just don't work right. We might make decisions and plan things, but actually getting going is something else entirely. Or, maybe it is our "fuel injectors" that have the problem, and maintaining the schedule is the hard part.

Leaders from all types of support groups say that it is common for people to feel great stress about not doing what they know they should. After these people realize they have a problem, they might make the decision to change their behavior. But then, just having made the decision can bring them such relief that they mistake their decision for action and never actually make the change!

Don't do that. Don't mistake intention for behavior; don't waste time waiting for inspiration. Godot is never going to come. Not today, not tomorrow, not next month. Remember that Beckett's play is considered "absurdist." Our waiting around for things to get better by themselves is absurdist too.

Homeschooling parents have made a huge commitment to their children—one that requires thoughtfulness, focus, energy, and discipline. If we are going to keep our commitment, we can't slack off. We need to get on with whatever plans or resolutions we made for our school or home this semester or year, and we'll feel the satisfaction of a runner in training—getting a little stronger, going a little further every day.

Hebrews 12:1-2a says, "...let us lay aside every weight, and the sin which doth so easily beset us, and let us run with patience the race that is set before us, looking unto Jesus the author and finisher of our faith."

See you at the finish line!

MAKING THE JOURNEY EASIER

DISTILLED *Life*

A number of years ago, my husband's parents both suddenly found themselves in need of care—one for Alzheimer's and the other for health-related issues. So one week we packed up their house. We looked through every single thing they owned, decided what we wanted to keep, decided what should go in a garage sale, decided what could be donated, and decided what to throw away. When we were finished, I cleaned the empty rooms, we left the keys for the new owner, and we walked away. It took us a mere three days to go through the house and decide the worth and future of their past.

The shock began when we first walked in. Everything was left as though they had been interrupted in the middle of life—which, in fact, they had. But also as if the interruption would someday end and they would come back—which they would not. Instead, they moved to their respective nursing homes, their lives each distilled down to one room.

Sorting through a household is tough. It is an emotionally painful, brutal task to assess someone's treasures and decide that a lot of it is junk and most of the rest they can live without. I came home and eyed my closets and drawers and possessions from a new perspective. It took less than ten minutes to fill my first trash bag.

So, now and then I ponder that intriguing question: if I had to move to one room or half a room, what are the things I would want with me?

How about you? What would you want with you?

Or, what if you had to distill your family life and

schooling down to the things that matter the most? Do you know what would you pick and why?

It really helps to occasionally look at your home and school from a "distilled down, one-room perspective" so you can get rid of any half-used, someday-I-might-get-to-it stuff, and focus on what matters.

Tip

Go through your rooms one at a time, one drawer at a time, one closet at a time, and see what you can throw away or donate. If you need inspiration, watching an episode or two of Hoarders ought to make you want to eliminate all your extra stuff!

ORGANIZATION

I hear many busy homeschool moms lamenting that their house is a mess. They complain they are too busy, don't have the energy, lack the will, don't have control over their kids, or some other reason.

But families don't thrive in chaos. Having a place for everything and cleaning up as you go can make a huge difference to a house. Building ten minutes into your schedule each day when *every member* of the house is required to put his or her things away can turn a messy, cluttered, unwelcoming home into a peaceful one.

I love to look at photos of interior designs and read about various design styles. One favorite design book is *Interior Design Master Class* by Carl Dellatora. One of the helpful ideas presented in it has to do with creating negative space. Simply speaking, negative space—the space between and around objects—helps define boundaries, show proportion, and provide relief from clutter.

One contributor, Salvatore Larosa, says we need to establish boundaries to concentrate attention on what matters. Jesse Carrier and Mara Miller add: "A space that is overly designed and weighted… lacks the necessary moments of visual relief that the eye requires in order to appreciate what it sees." And Campion Platt stated, "The space between things is just as important as the size of the objects themselves."

A common and related theme among many of the designers is editing. They want balance, clarity, and simplicity. Jane Schwab and Cindy Smith state, "When we edit, we ask ourselves if the object is congruent with our vision for the room."

That's a question to ask yourself: is your house congruent with your vision? I encourage you to do *whatever it takes* to make your home space cozy and inviting. Don't be helpless. Make house rules and enforce them. You've chosen to keep your kids home, so do your family a favor and make your home a place where you all really want to be!

I've noticed that whenever I return from any stay—in a stunning hotel room, a friend's cozy house, or a simple African hut—I come back and look at my home with fresh eyes based on what I've just seen.

Sometimes I'm just relieved to be back in a bug-free environment with clean water and a hot shower. Other times I look around and wonder if there's something we should change to improve things.

These are questions I ask: Does our home reflect what we really want? Is our space both welcoming (clean, nicely arranged) and useful (organized, tidy)? Do our furnishings, decorations, and landscaping create the atmosphere we want to project and enjoy? Do our collections look like clutter or is there enough "white space" there? Should I rotate something out—or maybe donate it?

We can ask similar questions about school, too. Is school reflecting what we really want? Is our curriculum working well for us? Are we focusing on what matters? Is our schedule still manageable (do we have enough space between events)? Did we want to keep the same activities or try something new?

We all need organization, whether we enjoy it or not. We have to create structure *and maintain it*. Homeschoolers need firm structure more than most because we're in charge of the household twenty-four hours a day. Look at your house, look at your schedule, look at your curriculum, look at your family. How is it going? Is everything okay, or do you need to redesign, de-clutter, and reorganize?

Tip

An organized life starts with an organized place. If you're struggling with getting everything done, first look at your home. Take a day (or two) off school and clean it up. Keep it cleaned up. Mess breeds mess, and the bigger the mess gets, the more hopeless everything feels.

Dads AND HOMESCHOOLING

"Let her go with us; she'll be okay," my husband said. I wasn't so sure. I took a quick photo of my family and our hosts as they started the climb, and then I quickly turned away. I didn't want my last memory of my six-year-old daughter to be one of her tumbling down the rocky face of the South Dakota Badlands.

That was many years ago now, and my daughter is still alive. My husband was right—most adventures don't end in a fall. Many years before that, he had also been the one encouraging our toddler son to climb on playground ladders while I cringed in concern. My husband's more adventurous nature brought a balance to my nurturing one. In fact, parenting, education, and other family life is a little like balancing a playground seesaw. Each parent needs to take an end in order for the seesaw to work.

The "dad part" of the homeschooling balance means different things to different people. In my own support group, we had dads who weren't at all involved in their kids' education, to dads who claimed the title "principal" and reviewed the work at the end of the day, to dads who actually did part of the teaching. Our group also dealt with issues brought about by absentee dads.

People have different ideas on exactly what dads can or should do, but they all agree on one thing—involvement. And the best advice for involvement might be summed up by Todd Wilson of The Familyman: *Don't assume. Find out what your wife needs from you.*

A dad's part of the seesaw balance might—or might not—have anything to do with classes. One of the biggest stress issues homeschooling counselors hear about doesn't even have to do with education—it is that moms are so busy with the teaching that they want help with time-management for "extra" things like *meals and laundry.* In those cases, "dads and homeschooling" might mean that dad cooks a couple times a week. In other cases, dad involvement might be the spiritual training of the children. Or it might be planning an adventure or working on projects with the kids.

I think the point is that homeschooling takes so much effort and dedication that it needs to be viewed as part of family life as a whole—not as an extra thing tacked on. So the best way dads can help us homeschool is to *help in the balance of family life*—whether by teaching some of the classes, organizing field trips, babysitting younger children, taking on the laundry, or maybe paying for a cleaning service once a month.

Dad, check with your wife. Help her keep up the practical home-life balance—the ride doesn't go anywhere with only one person on the seesaw.

Milk and Cookie Parenting

I remember, when my son was close to three, listening to my friends discuss the activities of their children the same age. Their kids were involved in things like swimming lessons, gymnastics, and "pre-science" trips. We didn't have a second car or any extra money. There was no way we could participate in those things. We played games, read, made stuff with Play-Doh, took walks to the playground. I was a little concerned: was my son missing out on something important?

One day I opened a magazine and was amazed—thrilled, even—to see an interview with Dr. David Elkind, professor of child development and author of *The Hurried Child* and *Miseducation: Preschoolers at Risk*. It wasn't a call to sign up our children for the latest program or sports camp. It wasn't a suggestion to enroll in early educational activities. Instead, the article talked about the stress children feel who have to start performing early and how negatively that affects them later in life. It was a plea to return to a relaxed attitude, something he called "milk and cookie parenting." Wow. By accident (or God's providence), I had been doing the right thing after all. What a relief!

Actually, I am a firm believer in activity-free time. You can call it boredom, if you want. When kids are bored or faced with free time, they become forced to use their imaginations; they research topics of interest to them and teach themselves new things. They draw and write and create. They invent games. They collect things. *They learn a lot all on their own*. I know because I was one of them. So were my siblings and the kids I grew up with. So were my kids.

Parents, don't be quick to fill every minute of your children's day—especially your young children. Don't sign them up for lots of extra lessons or activities or keep them out of your way with electronic baby sitters. Let them *find* something to do that requires their own imagination. Let them become problem-solvers. Let them collect something. Let them create. Let them explore. Let them play.

Relaxing INTO PRESCHOOL

So, what about preschool?

A man I knew whose wife just had a baby cornered me at his office and asked, "What curriculum should we consider so that our son can get into a great college?" Wow.

There are two things about your preschool children I'd like to say up front: The first is that it is important to give your children the freedom to be the people God made them to be. Yes, you need to expose them to every subject, but, just as you can't—*and shouldn't want or expect to*—turn willow trees into oaks, you can't force your artistic children to become mathematical geniuses (or the other way around).

The second thing is that we're dealing with preschool here. You don't have to start with all the

information your children will ever need to know in life. It is important to remember that "pre" means "before." Preschool children are not in school yet. This is the time to play with your kids, read to them, take them on field trips, and teach them skills at home.

You don't need a curriculum in order to teach colors—go for walks in your garden and point them out. You don't need a curriculum in order to teach counting—take your kids grocery shopping and count the items in your cart. You don't need a curriculum in order to teach measuring—bake cookies together. You don't need a curriculum in order to teach matching—sort socks from the clean laundry. You don't need a curriculum in order to teach shapes—hunt for shapes through the rooms in your house.

After all, one of the wonderful benefits of homeschooling is flexibility and the chance to tailor your school to your own children. So relax and just enjoy your kids. You can be assured that they are going to pick up the skills they need. Remember that these skills are like potty training: by the time your children get to college, no one will care how old they were when they mastered them!

THE *Adventure* OF HOMESCHOOLING

We all homeschool for different reasons. Some, because we just love the idea; some, because we're convicted that this is what we should do; and some, because we are trying to escape something we don't want from another school system. But, whether you are an enthusiastic homeschooler or a reluctant one, I urge you to look beyond the routine and tasks of homeschooling and embrace the *advantages* and *adventure* of it.

Homeschool parents get to choose their curriculum, the teaching style best suited for their kids, the number of field trips they take, the number of hours they do school, the time of day they teach, where they do their lessons, how they do their lessons, and with whom they do their lessons. No public or private school teacher gets those advantages.

Homeschool kids get one-on-one tutoring. They

can do schoolwork with their pets in the room or while standing or sitting...maybe even occasionally lying down. They can have classes or apprenticeships suited to their particular interests. They can take the time to immerse themselves while they explore new topics. They can skip some classroom work and learn while traveling.

One of my favorite ways to incorporate adventure into homeschooling is to use themes. While themes take some work for the parent to prepare, they save work in the end because you involve all your kids and many subjects at one time. Prepare a theme with another family, and you have half the work and double the fun!

Joe Dean of Quest Experiences explains the philosophy behind using themes in education. He asserts that, whether we realize it or not, our lives are represented in themes. If we are at home, we are surrounded by sights, sounds, and smells that tell us we are home. If we go on vacation where we hear the rustle of palm trees, smell the salty ocean, feel the sand squishing between our toes, and taste sweet pineapple, we learn about having a tropical experience. If we pack up our skis, coats, and gloves and head to snowy mountains, we learn what a winter experience is like. If we get ready for a hurricane by stocking up on batteries, water, and packaged food, we learn some survival skills. When we see crèches, packages, wreaths, lights, and trees with glittery balls in our stores and neighborhoods, we know Christmas is coming.

In fact, themes show us that seemingly random items and facts actually show relationships. So if life delivers information in collections or themes, it makes sense to try to represent educational information in a similar format.

Joe also asserts that our observations and engagement (hands-on activities) in the theme help the experience to become personal, which is why we still recall many of the details years later. A good example of this is a visit to a living history museum, where your kids get to taste the food, try the crafts, play the games, and feed and smell the barnyard animals. They'll remember much more about eighteenth-century life that way than if they read it in a book. The more developed the theme—the more someone is able to see, smell, feel, hear, taste, and do—the richer the experience, the greater the adventure, and ultimately the more vivid the memory. Isn't that what learning is about?

As a homeschooler, *you* have the authority to make school special. You can evaluate the curriculum, method, and pace for your children. You have multiple choices of how you spend each day. A world of options is at your fingertips. That is exciting!

The chore of homeschooling becomes the adventure of homeschooling when you look beyond the basics and explore the *possibilities*.

Tip

Be sure to look up Joe Dean's Quest Experiences online for fabulous adventure ideas. Research the children's activities at any historic site website, too—you can often duplicate those ideas at home. I once produced an entire Civil War adventure from interesting activities listed on a battlefield site. Fill in with ideas from Pinterest.

For field trip ideas, keep an eye on your county's calendar of events online. Some great books for planning trips are the *Kids Love* guides by George & Michele Zavatsky, which list places to explore in various states. Also consider the *One-Day Trips through History* by Jane Ockershausen for ideas when you're in the D.C. area.

STAYING *Focused*

I remember when we passed another milestone—starting on "college hunt number two." One would think we could have used the knowledge gained the first time around, but with different kids, we looked for different things, and so it was all new.

Saturday night we traveled home on winding country roads, illumined only by our headlights. With faint house lights the only thing showing through from the distance, our focus was absolutely and totally on the road. We couldn't see "the sights," or pick out too many landmarks, or see where other roads led; instead we had eyes just for the path we had chosen. It was interesting that, because the darkness didn't allow us to see far, it forced us to maintain our focus.

I see the homeschooling journey in a similar way. Each year, and maybe for each child, we look around, gather information, ask questions, pray, and then choose our path. At that point, in order to focus, all the other roads need to recede into the dark. We have to get used to that idea, because we need to understand that no matter what curriculum we use, or how many activities we do, there *will* be something left undone; your kids and mine will miss out on something, and it might even be something wonderful.

It's very simple: for every path we choose, there are hundreds more we didn't choose.

If that thought bothers you, ask yourself this question: Was my education complete at age eighteen? Was my character training complete by then? You and I know the truth, so why would we expect that in eighteen years we could provide every opportunity for education and character training for our kids? We can't. We're going to hit a lot, but we're going to miss some too. That's okay—our kids have a lifetime in which to discover, grow, and learn.

Maps show a lot of routes. Some are shorter, some more scenic, some lead through diversions, some offer no frills, some are well-traveled, some lonely. As long as you know your destination, they all get you there—but you have to make choices based on your priorities. The nice thing is that if you hit a roadblock, you can always go back to the map and try another way.

Practical SCIENCE

It is very clear that Jefferson's quote about all people being created equal does not apply in our family. I can't imagine having the mind of an engineer or inventor. I can't even imagine being a person who asks those questions that lead to inventions. If it were up to me, we'd still be living in caves. The caves would be pretty inside and have gardens outside. We'd have great discussions and lots of stories, but we'd be pulling our water from the stream and going to bed at dusk—I wouldn't have thought up candles, let alone electricity.

My kids are all artsy, too. Our family's lack of scientific imagination was brought home during one daughter's college physics class. We could not, for the life of us, figure out why she had to work so hard in an introductory course. We knew she wasn't going to be an astronaut! After a semester of plain hard work and perseverance, there was nothing left to do but get back at the teacher with our own problems:

Two parakeets fall from the same ledge at 10:53 a.m. on the equinox. They fall facing each other 10 cm apart at the rate of 10 m/s with no air drag. Both sneeze at the same time.

1. At what time do the sneezes meet?
2. How far will parakeet #2 have fallen below the sneeze of parakeet #1 when it crosses his trajectory?
3. What will the final speed of the two sneezes be upon impact?

An astronaut wearing no helmet coughs while riding a frictionless merry-go-round that is orbiting the sun at a distance of 3 AU. The merry-go-round is rotating counter-clockwise, and the astronaut is facing the outside.

1. When he coughs, will the rate of the turn a) remain the same, b) decrease, or c) increase, forcing the astronaut to fly off the merry-go-round?
2. What is the escape velocity of the cough?
3. How would wearing the helmet have changed the effect of the cough on the speed of the merry-go-round?

Santa carries his sack across the sky at constant speed. How much work does he exert on the sack if he calls to his reindeer at the same time?

On second thought, I think we have great scientific imagination.

Now if we could've just gotten a scientist to do something really useful like watch my daughters execute their pirouettes and fouettés and tell them how to correct the imbalance that prevented them from doing thirty-two in a row— that would truly have been worth something!

Living with Enthusiasm

Enthusiasm. Intensity. Those are two qualities my mother had in abundance and part of why people loved her and were fascinated by her.

You know, when you live with an enthusiastic person, every day can seem like an adventure. My mother would make faces in her roll dough when she finished kneading and chase us around the kitchen with it. She turned into sassy Brer Rabbit when she read us his stories at night. She passed on her delight when she pointed out "Moses in his basket" or "Jack in his pulpit" in her rock garden. She laughed with neighbors as she shared with them tubs of eggplant that came up where she thought she had planted zinnias. And she turned our dismal 5:00 am vacation departures into breakfast feasts in the car along with excited discussions of what animals we were going to see when we arrived at the game reserve.

Once, when we returned from boarding school, we discovered she had been working with the missionary nurses and doctors to put on a Winnie the Pooh play for us. It was quite a sight to see Dr. Bennett lumbering around on all fours as he played Eeyore; our renowned surgeon, Dr. Cook, up on a ladder-turned-tree, holding forth as Owl; and our lab technician's wife wandering around with an umbrella, saying, "Tut, tut—it looks like rain."

My mother turned our little Sunday School into missions adventures. When we saved up enough offering to help pay for a children's Bible book to be printed in Italian, she planned a huge spaghetti night and art show, and every single person on the mission station entered something for the display.

She was just like that. If you were going to do something, if you were going to even be alive, you might as well do it wholeheartedly and with enthusiasm. Her attitude didn't just affect our family; it spilled over to all our friends.

She impacted strangers, too. My mother wrote a column for her hometown newspaper all the years we lived in Africa, filling it with lively stories of the happenings at the hospital. People responded with packages of baby blankets, hot water bottles, and used clothes to be passed out. It was no surprise to any of us when she won the Distinguished Alumna Lifetime Achievement Award from Shenandoah University in 1992.

My mother died at age ninety-four. People from all over came to her memorial service and shared about her enthusiasm and her impact. They talked about all kinds of things— her sense of humor and the funny stories she told about her mishaps; her feisty, impertinent puppet Lucy; her piano playing; her great cooking and hospitality; how much she witnessed for the Lord; their enjoyment in attending the Bible study she taught in her retirement community.

Her legacy was not based on her deeds, but on her deeds performed with enthusiasm. *That* is what people responded to and remember. When she entered Heaven on February 1, 2017, my mother surely won the Distinguished Alumna Lifetime Achievement Award from God.

What about us? Will we also impact our families, friends, and neighbors by our enthusiasm? It's never too late to start.

SECOND CHANCES

At the end of a school year, you might find yourself sighing with satisfaction, sighing with relief, or sighing with longing to start up again. To paraphrase John Denver: "Some years are diamonds and some years are stones."

Chances are your year wasn't all sparkling jewels, but I hope it wasn't a "terrible, horrible, no good, very bad" one either.

There were times I couldn't quite figure out where mine fit. I remember one year that didn't go at all the way that I'd planned—programs and schedules all got upended in mid-fall when an elderly friend died and I had to dismantle her house in Canada. Just when I was catching up from that, Nutcracker and Christmas-program season started. Anyone with ballerina daughters will understand the rehearsals those entail. At that same time, and probably partly for that same reason, another disc in my back tore, and I spent the rest of the school year barely involved. Other people took over the driving and the programs, and I rested and went to therapy. It was not our typical year.

That wasn't the first time we had to make adjustments, though. There was the year I had a colicky baby, a new kindergartner, and a fourth-grader. One day my husband came home from work after another sleepless night, showing me he was wearing shoes from two different pairs. I laughed and laughed until I went to change my clothes: *I'd been wearing my pants backward all day!*

When my youngest was a toddler, she required so much oversight that I felt I wasn't doing a good job of teaching the other two children. Unless I pinned her clothes I'd find that she would paint the walls, windows, and carpet of her room with the contents of her diaper. One time she came downstairs extremely proud of herself for shampooing her own hair. It was a gloppy, soggy mess that dripped goo all over the house. Another time I found that she had carefully laid out every egg from our refrigerator in a perfect diagonal along the kitchen floor. She was one of those kids I really expected to have to call poison control for before she was grown. And in the meantime, we tried to get our schoolwork done.

One of my friends gave me some of the best advice I ever received about homeschooling: *never give up based on one or two difficult years; things will change.*

Most good things in life require fortitude—not just that college degree, marriage, parenting, or spiritual growth, but also becoming skilled at an instrument, learning a sport, finishing a sewing project, even taking care of a garden or teaching a bird to talk. Homeschooling is no different.

For some reason, we hope or expect our progress through life will be smoother than it usually is. It shouldn't surprise us when we encounter obstacles, but it often does and makes us panic, causing us to question our firm decisions. Yes, there are some circumstances that require or allow for a change of path, but when problems come, we need to remember why we made our decisions in the first place. *If the underlying truths haven't changed, our decisions shouldn't change.*

After all, there's something good that happens every summer—we get to start over. We get another chance to recharge our enthusiasm and determination, find answers to specific problems, and look at the latest curricula. We can compare notes on our less-than-perfect year with others and recover our sense of humor. We'll recognize that's just the way homeschooling is; the way life is.

As we've learned from the popular children's book about Alexander, even if this year really was terrible, horrible, no good, and very bad, it won't help to move to Australia.

Tip

If you are trying to teach older children while keeping a preschooler safe and happy, make him a busy box. Buy a plastic tub that is only ever opened during school when you most need to concentrate on your older children. Put a variety of things inside ahead of time and rotate them every day so that your child never knows what to expect. Ideas include coloring pages and colored pencils; stickers; puzzles; DVDs; small toys; construction paper with toddler scissors; Play-Doh; kinetic sand; sewing cards; beads; car mat with a couple cars; zoo or farm animals to set up, etc. Reminder: none of the things from your busy box should be available any other time or the box will lose its charm and usefulness.

KEEPING YOUR *Armor* CLEANED

There is something about the military that fascinates many people. Even families who don't allow guns in their homes find their little boys aiming sticks, fingers, or Lego weapons at imaginary enemies. We can't avoid it, and I finally decided I didn't want to.

What better forum to teach our kids about good vs. evil; about not "going down to Egypt" for help instead of calling on God; or about the dangers of trusting in horses and chariots instead of the One who sets up and brings down kings. Think of Psalm 18 or Ephesians 6, and there's immediate "scope for the imagination" using fortresses and armor.

There are other reasons I like warfare studies. One of my favorite scenes in Tolkien's book *The Two Towers* takes place in Rohan. Weary, loyal soldiers return from battle, thrilled to find their once-feeble king, Théoden, strong in mind and body, having shaken off the influence of an evil advisor. One by one his soldiers kneel before the throne, place their swords at his feet, and say, "Command me."

Have you ever wanted so badly to use your gifts, to place them at the feet of a king and be told, "This sword, this talent, is the very one I need!"?

Or maybe you feel the opposite—pretty comfortable, a little tired, preferring not to get involved? Remember what the Israelite tribes Gad and Reuben were told: to sit back is to discourage the rest of God's people—no one is to relax until the battle is won. Sun Tzu warns us in *The Art of War* that when we're battle-weary, all the enemy has to do is take advantage of it "as if he were setting a ball in motion on a steep slope. The force applied is minute but the results are enormous."

We're all at war—sometimes literally, but always spiritually. We have to protect ourselves and also teach our kids how to protect themselves. Sometimes the fight is against obvious ungodliness, but sometimes as parents and homeschoolers we also need to fight against fear, apathy, discouragement, anger, timidity, blame.

Take heart. We're all in this together, trying to quench those fiery darts. And, fellow homeschooler, you have a job to do—so keep your armor oiled and your sword clean; the King has picked it up. You have been commissioned.

ADVICE ALONG THE WAY

Thundering Displays

We stood in awe, looking over at falls so wide we could not see from one end to the other, even when we walked across the bridge into Zimbabwe. The rainy season was long over and the Zambezi River ran placidly, sometimes flowing as one river, sometimes separating into streams meandering along little islands. Suddenly it came to this large, sudden drop right into the earth. Mist rose from the force of the water hitting the gorge below. But the topography didn't look like that of any other great falls: the cleft in the land—cut by a giant "celestial axe" in the rock—simply swallowed the water. I thought it was an absolutely perfect picture of Revelation 12:15 and 16.

During the rainy season, Victoria Falls carries so much water that the mist obstructs the view. We've heard that visitors get so wet from the spray that they wear raincoats and find the slippery paths treacherous. The falls sound like their African name, "Water that Thunders." The only way tourists can really see them well at that time is by air.

Isn't that interesting! Those same things can often be said of any hustle and bustle. We homeschoolers can be like those falls: we usually get the "scheduling thing" down pat, and know how to pack it all in. We flow faster and wider, fall deeper, cover more ground, make more noise. We look and sound pretty spectacular. We work hard because we are creating our very own "world-heritage sites" in our children. Many times, to our relatives and acquaintances, our families even qualify as wonders of the world. It's not that we're trying to be impressive; we're simply trying our best to do the right thing.

But it's easy to forget that our fallout, our "spray," might be making life slippery for the very people we are trying to help—our children. Our "thunder" might not sound so inviting to them. And we don't notice that our wonderful display sometimes just ends up in the earth's cracks.

Maybe it's time for the aerial view. Today is a good day to stop, rest, ponder, and pray. We don't want to add to our homeschooling might. Rather, we want to evaluate each attitude and activity carefully and choose wisely so that we can control the flow.

SMOKING MOUNTAINS

One summer my family visited Pompeii. We had a great tour guide who took us all through the ruins, showing us homes with frescoes still visible on the dining room walls, restaurants with holes in marble counters where self-serve pots of food were placed, public steam baths, temples, and the market. He talked about the way the people lived and their sophistication and advancement—things like art that showed perspective long before the Renaissance masters came along, and courtyard designs that caught and funneled rainwater into below-ground reservoirs.

We also saw those famous casts of people covering their faces or turning away the moment the gases

and ash came down. One minute they were living normal lives; the next minute they became preserved in ash. How could that be?

Apparently the explosion was like a bomb, with the entire middle portion of the mountain blown out. What was once a cone shape now has jagged side peaks.

I asked the guide, "Weren't there any warnings at all?"

His answer surprised me. "Oh yes, the mountain had been smoking for a long time. The trouble was, the people just thought it was a pointy smoking mountain; they had never heard of a volcano so they didn't recognize the danger."

Can you imagine?

That made me think: We may have beautiful, advanced, sophisticated lives too. But, how many smoking, cone-shaped mountains might we also have? Maybe behavioral issues with our children that we don't deal with, or

One of the great benefits of belonging to a community—a church, a "watchdog" organization, or a homeschool support group—is that there are people there on the lookout for smoke; people who can identify moral, ethical, political, educational, behavioral, and health volcanoes and warn us of their danger.

Since none of us wants her family to end up looking like jagged peaks, it would be a good idea to pay attention to those who have traveled a little bit more and who can differentiate between morning fog and warning smoke—those who can recognize volcanoes for what they are.

learning problems that we overlook, or marriage concerns that we ignore...because we just expect it's natural that the mountain *should* smoke.

I, for one, don't want to be one of those people buried in ash who didn't understand the importance of the signs.

Thinking Like an Israelite

Not too long after we moved into our home, I began thinking like an Israelite. We had a lovely, brand new house and were working on the gardens, which were becoming beautiful and peaceful—a place for enjoying flowers and birds.

And then the house behind us was built, and the neighbors moved in.

Up until this time, we had thought of our home in terms of Psalm 16:5-6: "The Lord is the portion of mine inheritance and of my cup: thou maintainest my lot. The lines are fallen unto me in pleasant places; yea, I have a goodly heritage."

But with the arrival of the neighbors, the lot was not being maintained and the lines were no longer pleasant. The school staff had problems with their children, a town representative spoke to them about their yard, and the sheriff checked on their dog.

We tried being friendly, we tried being understanding, we tried being helpful, but eventually I became frustrated and angry. One day, I found myself saying to God, "*Why* did you give us this beautiful place *only to* bring these noisy, rude people right behind us!"

And then I laughed. I had just finished studying Exodus where complaining rather than asking was a serious issue. *Why* did you bring us here *only to* have us pursued by the Egyptians? *Why* did you bring us here *only to* have us die of thirst? *Why* this? *Why* that? It was obvious that whining was a problem with the Israelites, and yet here I was using the **exact same wording**.

So I changed tactics. No more whys or complaints. Instead, I asked God what He planned to do about the problem.

A contagious disease swept through the school. To keep their play set from being contaminated, the lady of the house decided she would never again welcome neighborhood children to her backyard. I was very surprised at her reaction to the sickness, but it eliminated a good portion of the noise and mess, and we could now actually have a phone conversation with our kitchen window open.

But the constantly barking dog was still an issue, so I again asked God how He would like to take care of the problem. He blessed the family. The husband got a nice raise, and they decided they wanted a bigger house—and moved.

We love our new neighbors.

I know God might not solve all my difficulties, but I know enough now not to whine. It's hard for me not to make suggestions, and it is very hard to wait, but I know He can do above all I can ask or think. I know His understanding of the situation and His imagination for a solution is obviously far above mine. After all, I wouldn't have thought of feeding a man by a raven, taking dips in water to cure leprosy, or blowing trumpets to take down a city wall.

What about you? Have you also learned not to whine or complain, but to ask? Have you taught your children the same? There is a huge distinction between the two, and the results are totally different.

Impacting the Culture

Recently, I saw a procrastination flow chart that I thought was pretty funny. The top box says, "Do Something Right Now." An arrow from that points down to the bottom box, which has just one word: "No." And there the flow ends.

Though I laugh at the sign, I do not want it to reflect me. I am quite sure that people who are out to change their world are not procrastinators. If you want to influence the culture around you, you don't slack off, you don't allow distractions, and you don't complain. Nehemiah is a good example. Why, he wanted to know, should he come down from rebuilding the Jerusalem wall to spend time with people who didn't even wish him well! Why should we?

Joseph is another example. In fact, I can't think of anyone I admire more. To do the best job he could in every circumstance, in spite of those circumstances—his very own brothers selling him into slavery, being given an unjust jail sentence, being forgotten by the very man he helped—is remarkable, admirable, almost unfathomable, and a sure way for the people around him to know that God was with him. Not only did Joseph affect the Egyptian culture, but he also saved the Israelite culture by refusing to hold a grudge.

Both of those men were slaves who did their jobs well, became noticed for doing their jobs well, developed relationships because they did their jobs well, and rose to prominence because they did their jobs well.

Now it's our turn. What will our story be? What will our children's stories be? We don't have to be in the national spotlight in order to influence the culture; our gifts don't have to be leadership or organization—we just have to work hard, with excellence, and with a good attitude right where we are. We have to reflect God. We have to teach that to our children, too. When we do that, His glory radiates out, and the culture sits up and takes notice.

Tip

Teach your children the "soft skills" they need to know for success. Things like a maintaining a positive attitude and counting their blessings rather than focusing on the negatives in life.

Teach your kids to have a strong work ethic. They need to work hard, put their phones away, ignore their e-mail and Instagram, and do what it takes to get the job done. That goes along with time-management skills. Teach your children to make lists of what needs to be done, get themselves up in the morning, know when assignments are due.

Communication and interpersonal skills are really important. Your kids need to know how to communicate clearly and listen intently, showing understanding, patience, fairness, and compassion in the way they talk to others. They need to practice good manners, which are simply commonly accepted standards that make everyone around us feel comfortable. Make sure they've practiced a good, strong handshake while looking people in the eyes.

Your kids need to be flexible—to follow someone else's way. Homeschooled children often begin to think that everything is flexible *their way*, and they should be able to have their say and help make the rules. At some point very soon they are going to run into college professors, sergeants, or bosses who demand things a different way. Along with that, children need the ability to accept constructive criticism. No employer or commander is going to say, "This is C work!" and leave it at that. They make you do something over and over until it is right. Make sure your children become the employees who can take constructive criticism and use it to improve their performance.

Above all else, talk to your children—all the time—about who is ultimately in control. God. Because He knows more than we do, He can make better decisions for us than we can. Our part is to do our best in all circumstances.

Journaling

It's very important for homeschool moms to keep our interests and hobbies alive to provide relaxation and remind us that we're not homeschoolers only.

Every few years I dig out my copy of *Markings* by Dag Hammarskjold and slowly sift through his musings on life. His is an interesting style of journaling. He doesn't record events; he talks to himself or about himself—sometimes just reflecting, often scolding. It's fascinating to go through his entries and ponder, "Do I agree? Can I relate? What happened to make him say that?"

Here is one to think about: "Dare he, for whom circumstances make it possible to realize his true destiny, refuse it simply because he is not prepared to give up everything else?"

There are also a few other special journals that I revisit. I go back and back to Sun Tzu's *Art of War*, which offers a fascinating set of rules that apply to all kinds of competitive situations. There are sticky notes, multiple underlining, and comments all over my book from my having used it as a resource in business, education, and even church programs.

I also return to *Out of Africa* by Isak Dinesen. I'm intrigued with the author's reflections and comments, some of which I might also wonder: "If I know a song of Africa—does Africa know a song of me? Would the air over the plain quiver with a colour that I had had on, or the children invent a game in which my name was, or the full moon throw a shadow over the gravel of the drive that was like me...?"

I like poetry that works as journal entries, too. Psalms are obvious ones. The wartime poems of Louis MacNeice also come to mind, as do Emily Dickinson's wry comments. How can you not nod and laugh along with her? "I felt a cleavage in my mind as if my brain had split; I tried to match it, seam by seam, but could not make them fit. The thought behind I strove to join unto the thought before, but sequence ravelled out of reach like balls upon a floor." (Life: CVI)

Do you journal? Keeping a journal—even if it is just to record favorite quotes from literature or the Bible—helps us track God's work in our lives. It says that we're well-rounded, interested readers and thinkers who have something to say and questions to ask about lots of topics—not just about our kids.

Maybe it's time to start a special journal just for you. Those blank pages offer a thrill of possibilities, begging for your thoughts, ideas, and questions.

Crumbling Stones

"Beloved Husband and Father.
Missionary Pilot.
They that wait on the Lord
will renew their strength;
They will mount up with wings like eagles."

The words, supposed to memorialize forever, were fading and the carving wearing thin, because in Southern Africa the sun is harsh, the paint is thin, and the stone is soft. Vines covered his last name. I found the stone only because I knew where to look.

I stood there, shocked. It was hard enough to be at his grave once more because a grave is such a final thing, the horrible fact made absolute and undeniable right in front of us. But this made it even worse: my father was being erased. It was a reminder that buildings crumble and flowers fade.

You know, curriculum choices and test scores will fade one day, too. Hours spent driving to classes or co-ops will be gone. Agonizing choices about college will be forgotten. Words such as "gifted" or "learning-disabled" will become meaningless.

But, our love of God and the love we bestow on our families is what will last long after we are gone. In my dad's case, his chiseling in my life is there to stay no matter what happens to the etchings on the stone.

If I hadn't made the journey just then, who knows if any future pilgrims could have even found my dad's grave. But I paid for the stone to be repainted and it looks like new. And there's a lesson in that too—it's not too late; time can be redeemed. God can restore the years that the locust has eaten (Joel 2).

So, if you are caught up in the very real—but little—worries of homeschooling, let me remind you: those carvings will one day all pass away and the stones will crumble. But the memory etchings in your family will last. If you need to work on those relationships to make some good memories, it's not too late for a little weeding and some restoration.

African BUSH

On a recent visit to the African bush, friends and I stayed at a private game reserve where animals came right up to our thatched cottage. The first morning there, a mom and baby kudu ambled past, vervet monkeys came to inspect, and a family of warthogs popped by. Even a warthog is cute when it stands right at the patio, watching and blinking, trying to figure humans out. Red- and yellow-billed hornbills and guinea fowl also stopped in and hung around as though they were expected to tea.

We had constant visitors. One night a bush pig came shuffling out of the veld to see what we were

having for supper. He stood there studying us over his long snout as though he were looking over reading glasses. He had a tiny string of a tail and altogether looked a defeated sort of fellow, but somehow that just made him endearing.

The third morning, one of the yellow-billed hornbills came and tapped at the glass door. When I went out to see him, there also stood a beautiful, majestic male antelope—an nyala. The nyala watched my movements curiously, his ears following the sound as I spoke to him. He stood there serenely and stayed for a long visit.

I was so excited for all of these close encounters.

It's a funny thing about the African bushveld. It is home to a lot of animals, and I grew up in it so I love it, but in a way it's kind of ugly—tufts of yellow grass, scrub bush, occasional aloes, and acacia thorn trees. It always looks the same. Unlike forests or jungles, it doesn't really fill in much over time, so whatever you see today looks pretty much as it did ten years ago, and will still look in another ten years' time.

So why do I bring all of this up? When I was sitting on the verandah, I saw animals come and go. In a one-minute period, a crested barbet might land and fly off again, a blue-headed lizard might scamper up a tree, or a mongoose might run by. There one moment but gone the next,

leaving no trace. Look away and you miss it.

It was a picture to me of the brevity of life. We, also, come and go, and the veld won't show much of a hint that we passed by. As the band Kansas used to sing, "All we are is dust in the wind…"

The only way to leave a footprint is to do something that has long-lasting impact.

I believe loving your children is one of those things.

High Places

One fall, my husband and I had the opportunity to visit Greece and Italy. Having just finished a Precepts study of Isaiah, I was struck by our guide's comment in Athens that "acropolis" means "high place." All over Greece we saw acropolises. While some of them may also have been used for defense, all of them had temple ruins for the worship of false gods.

Do you know what Israel was supposed to do with their high places? Tear them down and reclaim that land for God.

Reclaiming can be a tough thing. Sometimes we don't even realize something needs to be reclaimed. We might view our "homeschool pillars" as history, tradition, architecture—and don't notice that maybe they are crumbling ruins that should have been torn down. It's easier to preserve the culture and history of our choices than to tear them down, but God might want to use that space for something else.

So—reclaim. How do we know when to do that? Jeremiah 23:18 and 22 say we are to stand in the council of the Lord to know what is right.

As we reclaim our choices, we reclaim and redeem our time.

While touring St. Peter's Basilica in Rome, we saw an interesting statuary display of four figures. One figure is holding an open book—a Bible—and looks as though she is contemplating a passage she just read. I thought of Proverbs 9:10: "The fear of the Lord is the beginning of wisdom."

Behind the reader sits an angel pointing to an hour glass she holds, warning us that time is moving along.

Putting those statues together in the exhibit was a brilliant idea. Together they look like a picture of Psalm 90:12: "So teach us to number our days, that we may apply our hearts unto wisdom."

As an educator you read words of wisdom in various articles, you hear words of wisdom from friends, and you hear wisdom from convention speakers. Keep an open mind, listen to what they say, and then stand in the council of the Lord to find out if there is any area you need to reclaim.

ARCHITECTURE

What a thrill to visit Westminster Abbey and experience the beauty, majesty, and magnificence of its stained-glass windows, ornate carvings, and gilded furnishings. The impressive size and very style inspires worship—arched windows, huge columns, and vaulted ceilings with flying buttresses, all pointing up to the heavens. Goethe was absolutely right when he described beautiful architecture as frozen music. How very appropriate that Handel is buried here.

We were excited to visit the graves of all those famous monarchs of my history books—Mary; Elizabeth; Mary, Queen of Scots; Henry V...as well as the graves or commemorative plaques of others who contributed so much to the culture and building of this great nation—Shakespeare, Hopkins, Tennyson, Newton, Wesley, Churchill.

At one point, I was shocked to discover that, as I stood musing at the memorial of one favorite—Handel, I was standing right on the grave of another—Dickens. In a nearby wing, I read the large marker for David Livingston, significant to me because I, too, spent many wonderful years in Africa, and had known of him from early childhood.

Being a fan of both architecture and British history, my visit to the Abbey was, to me, an event! But the biggest understanding I came away with was the *continuity* of history. This is not just a bunch of people from the past collected in one building, but a demonstration that, in one way or another, the past builds the present and future. At the Abbey, there is no doubt—something important is happening here.

But not too far away, on a corner of Trafalgar Square, stands another church I was anxious to see. This one surprised me by how tiny and careworn and unassuming it was. Just by looking at it, one would think that perhaps the history and influence of this place would be fairly local. One would be wrong. It is St. Martin-in-the-Fields, world-famous for its outstanding music.

I sat in one of the old wooden pews for a few minutes and listened to the choir rehearsing for that evening's performance, and was forcibly reminded—it's not the packaging or size that counts; it's what you do with what you have!

That's true for homeschooling, parenting, and ministry too. Most of us are not abbeys with generations of history and the wealth of kings holding us up; our families are tiny churches, careworn and struggling to make ends meet. But, oh the music we can make! With God's help, we can use our resources, time, love, and practice to make beautiful music that swirls up and freezes into cathedral architecture that lasts the ages—architecture that, as Sir Christopher Wren said, "aims at eternity."

Pointing the Camera

Venice is one of my very favorite cities. You look one way and see gondoliers with their striped shirts and black pants rowing down canals, whistling and laughing with each other as they pass; you look another way and see pastel homes with arched windows and carved lintels and wrought-iron railings and window boxes spilling over with flowers.

Another direction, you walk along narrow cobblestone streets filled with shops selling decorated masks and handmade lace and blown glass, and see people chattering away happily in outdoor cafes.

Venture a distance in any direction and you will cross canal bridges and find yourself in a little square with a magnificent church, impressive pillars on the outside and spectacular paintings and gilding and statues and marble work on the inside.

You can row past the home of Marco Polo; visit the stunning mosaics, gorgeous domes, and winged lions of St. Mark's Cathedral; and attend a concert in the church of Antonio Vivaldi.

There is no place you don't want to aim a camera, no nook you don't want to explore. Even the tiniest alley boasts brick houses with old shutters, clay roof tiles, and interesting ironwork. Who cares if you get lost? This is *Venice*—a feast for the senses, the perfect field trip for the arts!

One time we had a funny experience.

We sat near the front of yet another beautiful church and listened enthralled to the chamber

ensemble Interpreti Veneziani's stunning performance of works by Vivaldi and other masters. What a lovely evening; what gorgeous music; what a perfect venue!

We wound our way back to our flat, popping over bridges carved with comical faces, strolling through mosaic-tiled streets, looking into shops laden with the trade of Venice. All of a sudden we came to water.

Water? This was supposed to be a street! We took a detour. Maybe something flooded and we could get around it. No matter where we turned, we finally realized that between us and our flat, we were going to be sloshing through streets filled with water.

The tide was in full. This wouldn't have been unusual in November, but then the city is prepared for it and puts up wooden platforms to walk on, but this was May and unexpected. There was nothing for it but to take our shoes off, roll up our pants, and wade through.

I started laughing. What a funny, down-to-earth end to a sophisticated evening. It reminded me of a statue I'd seen in Rome

of a large, stately lion bearing a firm, regal look, with wings unfurled and ready for action—only the effect was destroyed by a seagull sitting on top of his head.

And so our regal evening ended with us hobbling and splashing through St. Mark's Square, giggling from the cold water, and holding tightly to our belongings so they didn't get ruined.

Ever had an experience like that? Everything going well in your family and school and then something unexpected happens to "put you in your place." It's just another reminder that a dose of humility and a sense of humor are necessary ingredients for life.

Take it in stride—that's just one more place to point the camera.

FINAL THOUGHTS

Life After Homeschooling

Once when I came back from a trip, a retired missionary friend asked me, "Did you feel that you had any spiritual impact?"

I was a little startled at her question but had to honestly tell her no—the purpose of the trip was educational. I was in Portugal to lead hands-on discovery activities on U.S. History for children in American schools.

She surprised me by saying, "That's okay. God just wants *us* to be spiritual and do our best no matter what we're doing."

She was right. You wouldn't think sewing is a particularly spiritual enterprise, but Exodus 28:3 tells us that only those filled with the Spirit were to make priestly garments. We also read that the Lord chose Bezalel and "filled him with the Spirit of God, with wisdom, with understanding, with knowledge and with all kinds of skills to make artistic designs for work in gold, silver and bronze, to cut and set stones, to work in wood and to engage in all kinds of artistic crafts" (Exodus 35:32-34 NIV).

Many of the leading characters of the Bible were not originally preachers, prophets, or evangelists, but simply people living for God. Jacob was a farmer; Moses, a shepherd; Joshua, a military leader; Ruth, a widow; Daniel, a civil servant; Peter, a fisherman...

Homeschooling fits right in there too, as does whatever it is we will undertake after we finish homeschooling.

When we're about to embark on a new thing, we might think (as did some of those biblical characters) that we don't have a lot to offer. We might think we have used up what we had to offer. Or we might think we will be asked to offer something unusual and become afraid.

But the question God asked Moses when it was time for Moses to take on a new task was, "What is in your hand?" And then God used what was already in Moses' hand to perform miracles, even though it was a simple rod, a shepherd's tool

(Exodus 4-14).

Joseph also used what was in *his* hand—his administrative abilities. Those abilities led him to be named the overseer of a household as well as a jail. In turn, they led him into contact with Pharaoh's servants and then to Pharaoh himself. Joseph's use of his gift in smaller ways led to his gift being used in huge ways when he was appointed vizier of the whole country (Genesis 39-41).

So, those of us who are finishing up homeschooling need to consider our future work with that spiritual perspective. Look at what is in our hand, put it to a new use, and recognize that it is God's instrument wherever and however we serve. It's kind of exciting to look forward to a whole new ministry, mission, job, or quest. What will yours be?

Transitions

I smiled last week when I entered the kitchen and looked at the fridge. A glass was perched on top—an indication that my son was visiting. It's amazing that the sight can make me smile, though.

One of my worst days as a parent was the day my son and his new wife moved

halfway across the country. As they were about to leave, he started to put his glass on the fridge, suddenly remembered he wouldn't be there to use it again, and stuck it in the dishwasher instead. Watching the realization hit him that this was his last time at home just about broke my heart.

Transitions can be awful. When I was little, I used to pray for the Rapture the night before my parents dropped me off at boarding school after the holidays. But, since we were all still on Earth the next morning, we made the long, dusty drive up and down mountain roads to go back to school. We were sick with tension and distress the whole way there and while we unpacked. But, after waving furiously from the front door and then running around the back of the house to wave again as our parents drove slowly out of the gate and round the block to head home, it was relatively quick for us to adjust. After a sad evening, we were distracted by classes starting, friends playing, and daily routines. It was that transition time that was the worst.

Those of you with kids finishing up high school and heading to college, the military, or the workforce are facing transitions, too, and I know it is horribly difficult. But, it does get easier. You adjust; they adjust. And, though it really, really pains me to have to admit it, deep down we know it is normal and right for our kids to move on to the next thing.

It does help to put it in perspective. Once, when I mentioned to a Zambian pastor we know that we had just taken our daughter back to school, he said wistfully, "Isn't it wonderful that one of your children has the opportunity to go to college!" It made me change my focus. His children and those in much of the world might never have the opportunity. All three of my kids went. I missed them terribly when they were gone, but the fact that they *could* go was a blessing, and I needed to express thankfulness for their gain rather than focusing on my loss.

So now that you are finishing the academic race with your kids, may I also remind you: isn't it wonderful that your kids have gotten this far— *and you got them here!* Isn't it wonderful that they are healthy enough to go off, that they have opportunities to pursue and choices to make, and that they have the whole world in which to make an impact!

Homeschooling parents, you have successfully raised the next generation. Congratulations!

ACKNOWLEDGEMENTS

Thank you to HEAV's amazing president, Anne Miller, who asked me to take on a new writing and editing career as magazine editor and would not take no for an answer.

Thank you to HEAV's outstanding publications director, Maureen Bittner, who kept telling me I need to publish in more places than just the magazine.

A special thank you to Ashley Taylor of Ashley Taylor Creative for working closely with me during the layout and design process and creating a beautiful book! And to Jason Smith of Wootton Publishing for his guidance throughout this project. We made it!

Above all, thanks to God, because I fully acknowledge that it's only in Him that we live and move and have our being. (Acts 17:28)

In memoriam to Dr. Lionel Basney, who designed and coached me through a special independent study on essay writing in college. I wish I could thank you again and tell you that it is as an essayist that I found my voice.

ABOUT THE AUTHOR

Mary Kay Smith homeschooled for more than thirty-two years, teaching her own three children successfully from preschool to college and later other children for families who were dealing with serious sickness. Mary Kay works as a developmental editor for several organizations and authors and writes and produces original educational discovery programs for organizations and schools around the world. She has created over fifty programs for groups of fifteen to more than 400 in seven countries. She has edited *The Virginia Home Educator* magazine since 2003, written and published magazine articles on various educational topics, and published the memoir *Wings Over Zululand*.

Reflections

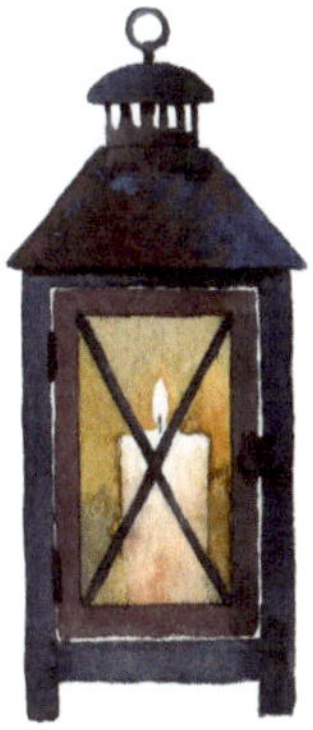

www.ingramcontent.com/pod-product-compliance
Lightning Source LLC
Chambersburg PA
CBHW041528220426
43671CB00002B/21